The Secret Life of the Woolly Bear Caterpillar

Illustrated by
Joan Paley

Laurence Pringle

BOYDS MILLS PRESS
AN IMPRINT OF HIGHLIGHTS
Honesdale, Pennsylvania

Bella walks in a jungle of grasses, clovers, and wild flowers. Hidden from sight, she begins a secret life.

Bella is no ordinary *caterpillar*. She is a banded woolly bear caterpillar, one of the most popular and beloved of all insects.

Bella's body is covered with black hairs (called *setae*) at her front and rear ends and a band of reddish-orange hairs around her middle. She looks fuzzy, but her setae are not soft to touch. They feel like the stiff bristles of a brush.

As Bella walks, her body undulates like an ocean wave. She seems to flow over the ground, but her walk is complicated. She moves sixteen legs of two different kinds!

Just behind her head are three pairs of *true legs* on her *thorax*, each tipped with a single claw. When Bella chews on a leaf, these six legs are good for holding the leaf steady. They also help her climb. The rest of her legs are *prolegs* on the rear part of her body, her *abdomen*. They support her body and help move it along. These stumpy prolegs have small hooks called *crochets* at their end that grip whatever is beneath Bella as she walks.

Bella grabs a clover leaf and begins to chew with strong, sharp *mandibles*. Behind the mandibles, on each side of her head, are six small eyes called *stemmata*. Bella's stemmata can't see details very clearly, but they can detect motion—and sometimes danger.

Something is moving quickly toward her! In an instant, Bella curls her body into a tiny ball and stays still. A garter snake slithers close and stops. Its forked tongue flicks in and out, in and out.

Since garter snakes don't usually eat hairy caterpillars, the snake moves on.

Bella uncurls her body and continues to search for food. She finds it with her keen sense of smell. Many tempting odors waft through the air. The meadow where her life began is a thicket of grasses, clovers, plantains, dandelions, asters, goldenrods, and more. To Bella, they all taste good.

Bella may be a tiny caterpillar, but she has a big appetite. Day after day she eats and eats and eats. Wherever she feeds, she leaves caterpillar droppings, called *frass*. At night or when it rains she rests in a sheltered place.

One day Bella stops eating. She lies still and bends her head. From the *spinneret* on the bottom of her head, Bella lets out some silk. She spins a mat on the ground, then hooks the ends of her legs onto the mat, holding tight. Her body begins to quiver, and her *exoskeleton* splits open.

Bella is molting. She wiggles and wriggles and writhes, breaking free of her old body. She even sheds the exoskeleton of her old head! Her new, bigger head is brown at first, then darkens as it hardens. She walks away as a bigger woolly bear, with a wider reddish-orange middle than before. But one thing has not changed: she is HUNGRY.

As summer days pass, Bella molts three more times. Each time she grows bigger. Each time more of the middle of her body becomes reddish-orange.

Living on the ground in a jungle of meadow plants, Bella's life is still a secret. No human sees her, though nearby wild creatures might. She walks past ants, sow bugs, and field crickets. She eats near grasshoppers, stinkbugs, and spiders.

One cool September morning, Bella is startled by a sudden shadow.

Bella feels herself lifted off the ground. A blue jay holds her tightly in its beak. The jay could swallow Bella whole. But something about Bella—perhaps the bristly feel of her body—stops the bird. It drops Bella and flies off.

Bella stays perfectly still, curled up. Then, when it seems safe, she uncoils. She lifts her head to sniff the air. Ah, some tasty leaves ahead. She hurries toward them.

As autumn days pass, Bella's world changes. The air grows colder, especially at night. Sometimes in the morning she lies still and warms her body with the energy from the rising sun.

As some leaves change color and fall to the ground, Bella searches for green leaves to eat. After two months of life, she is nearly two inches long, with a broad band of reddish-orange hairs around her middle.

Then, she stops eating, and sets off on a journey.

Bella walks for days, through a small forest and across lawns and gardens. Each night she curls up in a hideout, then begins to explore again. It is now, when she's a good-sized caterpillar and on the move, that she's most likely to be seen by people.

She reaches a wide, barren space. As she begins to cross, something huge rushes toward her! It roars overhead, then disappears. WHOOSH! A swirl of wind ruffles Bella's hairs.

She keeps walking. She does not know about the danger of streets and cars—but someone does. Fingers grab Bella, and pick her up. Nestled in the palm of a hand, she is carried safely across the road and set down gently in a field. Left alone, she waits, then uncurls her body and begins to walk again.

At the edge of the field a rocky wall rises in front of her. There, Bella finds what she has searched for—a secret, safe shelter. She curls up under some dead leaves and stays there, day and night, all through the winter.

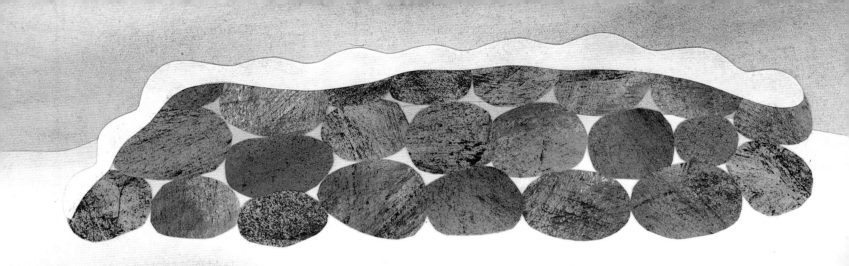

Snow covers the stone wall. Within Bella's body, a chemical called *glycerol* keeps ice from forming in her cells. Frosty winds may blow, but Bella is asleep, alive, and well.

In the warming days of spring, Bella awakens but moves very little. She waits and waits until grasses, dandelions, and other spring plants sprout and grow. Only then does she leave the stone wall and begin to eat.

She feasts for a few days, then hides in an open space among the stones. There, using the hairy setae from her body and silk from her spinneret, she weaves a *cocoon* that encloses her whole body.

Inside the cocoon, Bella molts one last time. This time, however, she changes into a smooth, shiny *pupa*.

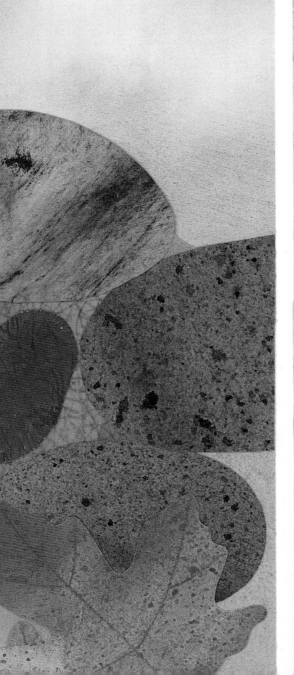

Inside the pupa, amazing changes happen to all of the cells that once made up Bella's caterpillar body. An adult moth's body begins to take shape. All of these changes are secret, hidden from sight inside her cocoon that is hidden in the stone wall.

On a warm spring evening, the cocoon begins to jiggle and shake. It opens on one end, and an adult moth crawls out. Once free, it holds onto the cocoon as its wings spread, dry, and become strong.

Then the moth walks out into the open. With the very first beat of her wings, she lifts off the ground and flies into a starry night sky.

Bella's life as a woolly bear egg, caterpillar, and pupa is over. Now she begins a new kind of life as an adult Isabella Tiger Moth.

In the nights to come she will sip nectar from flowers, find a mate, and then lay a cluster of pearly eggs. Within each egg will develop a banded woolly bear caterpillar. From each tiny egg, a tiny caterpillar will wriggle out. And each one will be ready to start its own secret life.

More About the Banded Woolly Bear Caterpillar

The word "caterpillar" comes from an ancient French word that means "hairy cat." A caterpillar is the *larva* of a moth, butterfly, or skipper. When a woolly bear caterpillar emerges from its egg, it is no more than a quarter of an inch long. It is also pale, but soon darkens.

When a woolly bear senses danger, it curls into a ball, head facing tail, and "plays dead." A false alarm, such as a gust of wind that shakes nearby plants, can cause the caterpillar to coil up. This "ball" of bristly reddish-orange and black setae discourages birds and other predators. Most insect-eating birds avoid "hairy" caterpillars. Also, the reddish-orange middle of a woolly bear is a warning. The bright colors of certain caterpillars, butterflies, and poisonous frogs "advertise" that the animals may taste bad, and may be harmful to eat.

Each time a caterpillar molts, a larger caterpillar of the next *instar* is formed. A woolly bear normally has five instars. After its next-to-last molt, the caterpillar begins its "walkabout," searching for an ideal place to overwinter. No one knows how a woolly bear chooses one place and not another.

Fall is the time in a woolly bear's life when it is likely to be seen by people, all across the U.S. and Canada. The caterpillars are usually harmless to pick up, although they may cause some people to have an itchy rash. They should be quickly released, because they are searching for a shelter where they can survive the winter.

Woolly bear cocoons, a blend of silk and body hairs, are a brown color, and about an inch-and-a-half long. When a moth first emerges from its cocoon, its wings are small and floppy. The moth pumps blood from its body into veins of its wings. The wings expand and spread out to normal size, but need about two hours to become firm and strong enough for flight. The wing span is about one-and-a-half to two inches.

The Isabella Tiger Moth is one of nearly 300 tiger moth species in North America, north of Mexico. In the southern parts of its range, this moth may have two generations in the span of twelve months—one in the summer, and one in which the caterpillar has a long life, through the fall and winter, then part of spring of the next calendar year. In 1797 a man named John E. Smith officially named this species *Phalanea isabella*. Now it is *Pyrrharctia isabella*. Smith chose the name "isabella" because of the moth's color. Long ago, "isabella" was a name for a brownish-yellow color.

Can Woolly Bear Caterpillars Predict Winter Weather?

Some people believe that woolly bear caterpillars predict winter weather. If they see a woolly bear with a wide mid-section of reddish-orange hairs, they say a mild winter is coming. Less reddish-orange and more black means that the winter will be a tough one. (Some believe the opposite is true!)

This idea is celebrated in certain towns that hold autumn woolly bear festivals. One is in Banner Elk, North Carolina, which holds the "Running of the Worms." (In some areas, woolly bears are called "woolly worms.") The winner of a series of caterpillar races "predicts" the coming winter weather. Other woolly bear fall festivals are held in Vermilion, Ohio; Beattyville, Kentucky; and two towns in Pennsylvania (Lewisburg and Oil City).

Scientists who study woolly bears know that the amount of reddish-orange on a caterpillar has nothing to do with the prediction of future weather. When caterpillars hatch from their eggs, each one can have different amounts of reddish-orange hairs, and some don't have any black bands at all. Also, woolly bears become more reddish-orange each time they molt. When food is plentiful, the time between the caterpillar's molts is shorter than when food is scarce. All of these natural factors can affect the appearance of a woolly bear. None have anything to do with predicting weather. That idea is a myth.

More About the Banded Woolly Bear Caterpillar

The word "caterpillar" comes from an ancient French word that means "hairy cat." A caterpillar is the *larva* of a moth, butterfly, or skipper. When a woolly bear caterpillar emerges from its egg, it is no more than a quarter of an inch long. It is also pale, but soon darkens.

When a woolly bear senses danger, it curls into a ball, head facing tail, and "plays dead." A false alarm, such as a gust of wind that shakes nearby plants, can cause the caterpillar to coil up. This "ball" of bristly reddish-orange and black setae discourages birds and other predators. Most insect-eating birds avoid "hairy" caterpillars. Also, the reddish-orange middle of a woolly bear is a warning. The bright colors of certain caterpillars, butterflies, and poisonous frogs "advertise" that the animals may taste bad, and may be harmful to eat.

Each time a caterpillar molts, a larger caterpillar of the next *instar* is formed. A woolly bear normally has five instars. After its next-to-last molt, the caterpillar begins its "walkabout," searching for an ideal place to overwinter. No one knows how a woolly bear chooses one place and not another.

Fall is the time in a woolly bear's life when it is likely to be seen by people, all across the U.S. and Canada. The caterpillars are usually harmless to pick up, although they may cause some people to have an itchy rash. They should be quickly released, because they are searching for a shelter where they can survive the winter.

Woolly bear cocoons, a blend of silk and body hairs, are a brown color, and about an inch-and-a-half long. When a moth first emerges from its cocoon, its wings are small and floppy. The moth pumps blood from its body into veins of its wings. The wings expand and spread out to normal size, but need about two hours to become firm and strong enough for flight. The wing span is about one-and-a-half to two inches.

The Isabella Tiger Moth is one of nearly 300 tiger moth species in North America, north of Mexico. In the southern parts of its range, this moth may have two generations in the span of twelve months—one in the summer, and one in which the caterpillar has a long life, through the fall and winter, then part of spring of the next calendar year. In 1797 a man named John E. Smith officially named this species *Phalanea isabella*. Now it is *Pyrrharctia isabella*. Smith chose the name "isabella" because of the moth's color. Long ago, "isabella" was a name for a brownish-yellow color.

Can Woolly Bear Caterpillars Predict Winter Weather?

Some people believe that woolly bear caterpillars predict winter weather. If they see a woolly bear with a wide mid-section of reddish-orange hairs, they say a mild winter is coming. Less reddish-orange and more black means that the winter will be a tough one. (Some believe the opposite is true!)

This idea is celebrated in certain towns that hold autumn woolly bear festivals. One is in Banner Elk, North Carolina, which holds the "Running of the Worms." (In some areas, woolly bears are called "woolly worms.") The winner of a series of caterpillar races "predicts" the coming winter weather. Other woolly bear fall festivals are held in Vermilion, Ohio; Beattyville, Kentucky; and two towns in Pennsylvania (Lewisburg and Oil City).

Scientists who study woolly bears know that the amount of reddish-orange on a caterpillar has nothing to do with the prediction of future weather. When caterpillars hatch from their eggs, each one can have different amounts of reddish-orange hairs, and some don't have any black bands at all. Also, woolly bears become more reddish-orange each time they molt. When food is plentiful, the time between the caterpillar's molts is shorter than when food is scarce. All of these natural factors can affect the appearance of a woolly bear. None have anything to do with predicting weather. That idea is a myth.

Glossary

Abdomen—the rear part of an insect's body, behind its thorax.

Caterpillar—the larval stage of a moth, butterfly, and skipper.

Cocoon—a shelter made by a moth larva, protecting the last-instar larva, and later the pupa that develops within.

Crochets—small hooks on a caterpillar's prolegs that help it grasp objects.

Exoskeleton—the outer body wall of an insect, crab, or other jointed, hard-bodied animal.

Frass—solid or semi-solid body waste of caterpillars.

Glycerol—an anti-freeze substance inside woolly bear caterpillars that enables them to survive cold temperatures.

Instar—another name for a caterpillar as it grows and molts several times. The caterpillar that hatches from an egg is the first instar. When it molts, a second, bigger instar forms. A woolly bear normally has five instars.

Larva—A larva hatches from an insect egg, and is the second stage of the four-stage life cycle of some insects. Some fly larvae are called maggots and some beetle larvae are called grubs. Moth, butterfly, and skipper larvae are called caterpillars.

Mandibles—hard chewing mouthparts of caterpillars that grasp and cut off parts of leaves, fruits, stems, and other plant parts.

Molting—in caterpillars, the process of shedding a tight-fitting "outer skin" to emerge with a new larger one. When the skin—called an exoskeleton—is new and soft, a caterpillar takes in air to puff it up. Once the exoskeleton hardens, there is room inside to grow.

Prolegs—stubby, simple legs on the abdomen of a caterpillar that have hooklike crochets.

Pupa—a pupa forms from a larva, and is the third stage of the four-stage life cycle of many insects.

Setae—stiff, bristly "hairs" on the body of a caterpillar.

Spinneret—a single tube that streams silk from silk glands inside the head of a caterpillar. Spiders have many spinnerets that are located at the rear of their body.

Stemmata—small, simple eyes of many insect larvae.

Thorax—the body region between the head and abdomen bearing the true legs, and wings of insects that fly.

True legs—the front six legs of a caterpillar that are attached to the thorax behind its head. Each leg has several jointed parts and is tipped with a single claw.

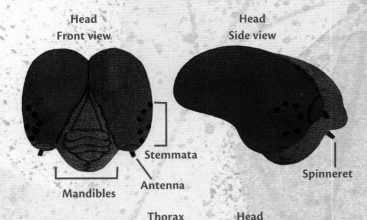

Head
Front view

Head
Side view

Stemmata

Mandibles

Antenna

Spinneret

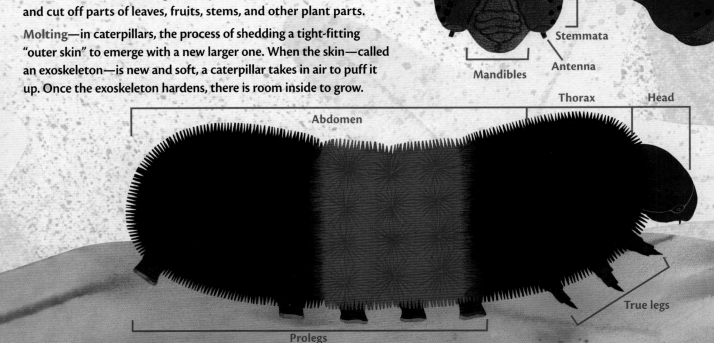

Thorax

Head

Abdomen

True legs

Prolegs

To Gail Langer Karwoski,
already a good writer when we met at Chautauqua in 1995,
a loyal friend ever since.
—LP

To a Special Someone, who cherishes family and beloved pets, dear friends,
each day, nature's inspiration; who wonders, thinks, dreams, creates and
builds; who embraces hard work, honor, truth, standing up, doing the right
thing, and holding dear a remembrance from childhood, which is, "you
can be or have what you wish if you set your mind to it."
You are celebrated.
—JP

The publisher thanks David Adamski, PhD, Department of Entomology, National Museum of Natural History,
Smithsonian Institution, Washington, DC, for reviewing the text and illustrations for this book. For verifying
specific details and information, the publisher also thanks John E. Rawlins, PhD, Curator and Chair of the
Section of Invertebrate Zoology, Assistant Director of Research and Collections, and Interim Co-Director of
the Carnegie Museum of Natural History; and John Calhoun, Research Associate at the McGuire Center for
Lepidoptera and Biodiversity at the Florida Museum of Natural History of the University of Florida.

JUN 1 8 2014

BOYDS MILLS PRESS
An Imprint of Highlights
815 Church Street
Honesdale, Pennsylvania 18431

Printed in Malaysia
ISBN: 978-1-62091-000-9
Library of Congress Control Number: 2013947716

First edition
The text of this book is set in Cronos Pro.
The drawings are done in cut paper and mixed medium.

10 9 8 7 6 5 4 3 2 1

FSC
www.fsc.org
MIX
Paper from
responsible sources
FSC® C012700